NORTHERN LINE
EXTENSIONS

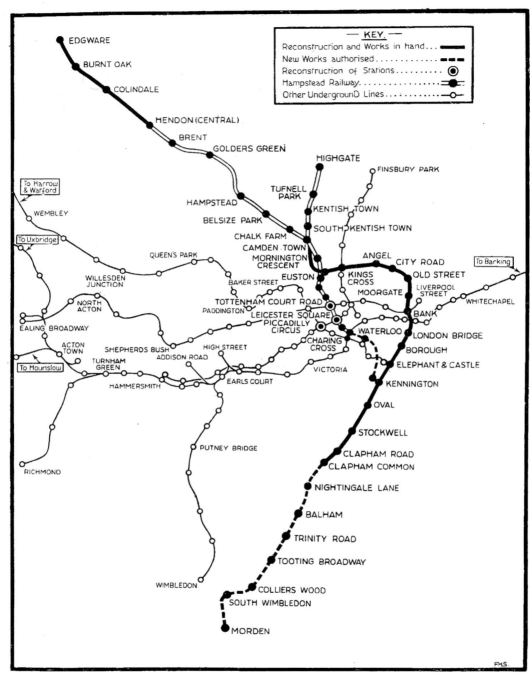

EDGWARE
BURNT OAK
COLINDALE
HENDON (CENTRAL)
BRENT
GOLDERS GREEN
HIGHGATE
FINSBURY PARK
TUFNELL PARK
HAMPSTEAD
KENTISH TOWN
BELSIZE PARK
SOUTH KENTISH TOWN
CHALK FARM
CAMDEN TOWN
MORNINGTON CRESCENT
ANGEL
CITY ROAD
QUEEN'S PARK
EUSTON
KINGS CROSS
OLD STREET
To Harrow & Watford
WEMBLEY
WILLESDEN JUNCTION
MOORGATE
LIVERPOOL STREET
To Uxbridge
To Barking
BAKER STREET
TOTTENHAM COURT ROAD
NORTH ACTON
PADDINGTON
LEICESTER SQUARE
WHITECHAPEL
EALING BROADWAY
PICCADILLY CIRCUS
BANK
WATERLOO
LONDON BRIDGE
ACTON TOWN
CHARING CROSS
BOROUGH
SHEPHERDS BUSH
HIGH STREET
To Hounslow
TURNHAM GREEN
ADDISON ROAD
ELEPHANT & CASTLE
VICTORIA
HAMMERSMITH
EARLS COURT
KENNINGTON
OVAL
STOCKWELL
RICHMOND
PUTNEY BRIDGE
CLAPHAM ROAD
CLAPHAM COMMON
NIGHTINGALE LANE
BALHAM
TRINITY ROAD
TOOTING BROADWAY
WIMBLEDON
COLLIERS WOOD
SOUTH WIMBLEDON
MORDEN

FHS.

DIAGRAM OF NEW WORKS UNDER CONSTRUCTION AND AUTHORISED.

NORTHERN LINE EXTENSIONS

GOLDERS GREEN TO EDGWARE 1922–24

SIMON MURPHY

TEMPUS

Frontispiece: The extension to Edgware was planned as one of a number of major projects for the Hampstead and City & South London Railways between 1922 and 1926, with a total budget of £12million. This map shows the Edgware line in the context of the other improvements.

First published 2005

Tempus Publishing Limited
The Mill, Brimscombe Port,
Stroud, Gloucestershire, GL5 2QG
www.tempus-publishing.com

© Simon Murphy, 2005

The right of Simon Murphy to be identified as the Author
of this work has been asserted in accordance with the
Copyrights, Designs and Patents Act 1988.

British Library Cataloguing in Publication Data.
A catalogue record for this book is available from the British Library.

ISBN 0 7524 3498 5

Typesetting and origination by Tempus Publishing Limited.
Printed in Great Britain.

Contents

Acknowledgements

Thanks are due to my colleagues at London's Transport Museum, especially David Bownes, Anna Rotondaro, Hugh Robertson and Samantha Ratcliffe in the Photo Library for their support, encouragement and pictures, and Oliver Green and Mike Ashworth for advice and information.

Special thanks to Chris Mawson at Simmons Aerofilms, and to Charlotte Cooper, as always.

Golders Green to Edgware

Extending the Northern line, 1922–24

As a child growing up in Hendon, North London, in the 1970s, I had little awareness of the Underground. Although my family lived within a mile of two Northern line stations, we travelled mostly on buses, and mostly to and from Kilburn and Paddington, for shopping or to visit relatives. I remember an epic family outing on the Tube to Aldgate East to visit a couple my parents had met on holiday in Bulgaria, in around 1975. I sensed my parents' unease on the system, although they had lived in London for twenty years. This might make them sound parochial, but the Tube just did not go anywhere they wanted to go. If we had lived in Neasden, the story might have been different but, as things were, I was left alone to rediscover the Underground as a teenager.

You could say I was attracted to the Underground for the same reasons my parents ignored it. I viewed the Northern line exclusively as a means to get out of NW4 on a regular basis, to visit school friends in East Finchley, to explore the West End, buy records, see bands and play Space Invaders; later to visit cinemas and art galleries. I remember one dull Christmas I felt the urge to escape especially keenly, but was crushed to find Brent Cross station dark and grey and closed – on Boxing Day! I loved the speed and comfort of the Tube, the 1938 Stock trains – red outside and warm green inside – zipping me down to the counter-culture mecca of Camden Town for second-hand records and books, and to Tottenham Court Road to window-shop for guitars and hi-fi. It was before the Travelcard era, but the child-return fares were cheap. The Red Bus Rover ticket was more economical, but given a choice I would always take the train.

I started working for London's Transport Museum in 1988, cataloguing glass plate negatives from the 1920s, in the electricity substation close to Hendon Central station. Some of the images in this book passed through my cotton-gloved hands on fragile plates of glass at that time, as I examined and described each one in detail. It would be more than an exaggeration to say that I resolved all those years ago to one day compile a book of these photographs, yet some of these images have lodged themselves in my memory and stayed with me since then, giving me an unusual perspective on the history of this part of London. Anonymous photographers working for the agency Topical Press took most of these photographs, recording the day-to-day activities of the Underground Group, and its successor, London Transport, from 1920 till the end of their contract in 1957. As you will see, every step of the Edgware extension project was photographed. In a more acronym-friendly period it would have been called the EEP, but the work was also part of a larger project to link the Hampstead Tube to the reconstructed City & South London Railway at Euston, also completed in 1924. The merged railways were renamed the Northern line in 1936.

It is hard to imagine these North London suburbs without the Underground. As a child I naturally assumed it had all been there forever, and apart from a dim awareness of London's inter-war growth that I knew included the streets I grew up on, this impression was not really dispelled until I started cataloguing those negatives in Hendon in the late 1980s. I was amazed by the emptiness of the landscape north of Golders Green in 1922. Posters were produced in large numbers to tempt city dwellers to sample the delights of what they called 'London's Country' in the 1920s, and the open land at the end of the Hampstead Tube fitted the bill nicely. In 1923 the tube extension arrived at Hendon, and continued on to Edgware a year later; the spell was broken in an alarmingly short time.

Golders Green had, from the beginning, been considered only a temporary terminus for the Charing Cross Euston & Hampstead Railway, known more comfortably as the Hampstead Tube. Even before the original line was completed in 1907, an extension to Edgware had been approved by Parliament. A further Act of 1912 allowed the London Electric Railway (LER) to absorb both the existing line and its extension plan – the Edgware and Hampstead Railway. The work did not, however, begin for another ten years, as it was delayed by the onset of war and financial troubles at the LER. The opening pages of this book show Golders Green in the intervening period, while the last section shows the stations as they looked in 2001.

The Underground Group (of which the LER was only a part) had not diversified into property in the style of the Metropolitan Railway, but the energy and effort they put into promoting Edgware as a new and perfect suburb would surely have led many to suspect otherwise. Perhaps they reasoned that promotion of the terminus amounted to promotion of the whole line, but in any case, their efforts were a great success. Alongside the photographs I have included some of the posters and advertisements that contributed to that success.

Although Hendon and Edgware were well established, with a combined population of almost 60,000 in 1921, and were already served by the Midland Railway and Great Northern Railway by the time the work in this book was begun, the land between them and Golders Green was almost empty. The ensuing decade would see the population of Hendon and Edgware rise by 95 per cent, spilling out to fill almost every acre of space along the 4.7 miles of the extension.

Copies of most prints reproduced in this publication may be purchased by writing to the address below and quoting the reference number in square brackets at the end of each caption. Personal visits to view the photographic collection, which covers all aspects of London's public transport, can be made by appointment. As most of the photographs are taken between 1922 and 1924, they are not individually dated, but are presented in chronological order. Many have been scanned directly from negatives that have never been printed and, while some show signs of deterioration, I trust this will not affect your enjoyment.

Simon Murphy, Curator (film and photograph collections),
The Photo Library, London's Transport Museum, Covent Garden, WC2E 7BB
http://photos.ltmcollection.org. http://www.ltmuseum.co.uk
Tel: 0207 379 6344

one

Golders Green and Beyond, 1906–1922

Golders Green in 1906, months before the opening of the railway. Carriages are visible on the extreme right. The district had only 100 houses at this time. The large estate agents' signs hint at the future. [1998/84463]

Golders Green station, not long after opening in July 1907, and before the completion of the forecourt and bus station areas. [2000/23065]

Opposite: The illustration at the top of this 1909 poster gives a reasonable idea of the Golders Green area at this time, as well as providing the prototype for Underground suburban promotion strategy for the next twenty years.

SOME OF
LONDON'S·CHOICEST·SUBURBS

LIVE AT	STATIONS	JOURNEY TIMES	FARE	STRIP TICKET RATE (6 TICKETS)
HAMPSTEAD	Bank and Hampstead - -	22	3d.	-
	Charing Cross and Hampstead	16	3d.	1/4
	Piccadilly Circus & Hampstead	16	3d.	1/4
GOLDERS GREEN	Bank and Golders Green -	26	4d.	-
	Charing Cross & Golders Green	20	3d.	1/4
	Piccadilly Circus & Golders Green	20	3d.	1/4
HENDON	Charing Cross and Hendon -	37	4d.	-
	Euston and Hendon - -	31	4d.	-

For further particulars apply at the Bookstall for a copy of "Healthy Homes." (Price 1d.)

SERVED BY
THE·HAMPSTEAD·R^{LY}

JOHNSON, RIDDLE & C? L?? LONDON, S.E.

ST JAMES' PARK STATION OFFICES, S.W.

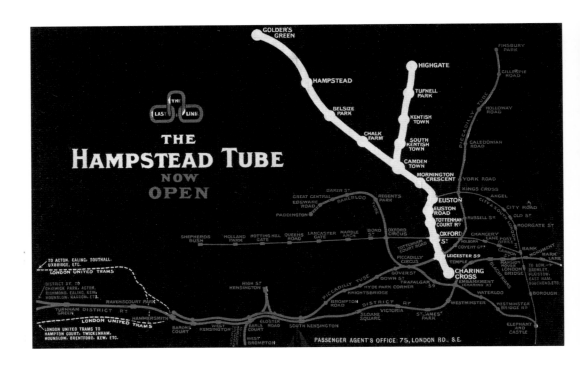

GOLDER'S GREEN

FOR HEALTHY HOMES···

THROUGH TICKETS EVERYWHERE

CHARING CROSS (FOR PLEASURE)		BANK (FOR BUSINESS)
3ᴰ	SINGLE FARE	4ᴰ
19 MINS.	TIME ON JOURNEY	25 MINS.
6 MINS.	TRAIN INTERVALS	6 MINS.
12·55 A.M.	LAST TRAIN OUT	12·30 A.M.

"** HAMPSTEAD VILLAS KIND DEFENCE FROM NOISE AND CROWD, FROM DUST AND DRAIN."

JOHNSON RIDDLE & C.º L.ᵗᴰ LONDON S.E.

Opposite above: An early Hampstead Tube map of 1907, showing links with the other early tube railways. Railway company names were frequently clumsy composites of other names at this time. In this case the Charing Cross, Euston and Hampstead Railway was shortened to the Hampstead Railway, or more usually, the Hampstead Tube.

Opposite below: Platforms at Golders Green in 1911, with a 1906 A gate tube stock train, ready for its return trip to Eustontube. [1998/75610]

Left: A 1910 poster, giving fares, journey times and train intervals to back up the vision of suburban bliss provided in the illustration.

Above: Early Underground staff in suits and wing collar shirts in the booking office at Golders Green, *c.*1912. Such staff did not wear uniforms at this time. [1998/88607]

Left: A postcard showing Golders Green bus station on Whit Bank Holiday in 1913. A written message gives the time as about 12.30 a.m. and the added annotation indicates 'Hendon on left, Hampstead on right'.

Golders Green station from the air, 1920. Note the expansion of housing compared to the 1906 view, and the word 'Underground' planted in the flower bed. [Simmons Aerofilms]

The Finchley Road entrance to Golders Green station in November 1921. The terminus buffer stops of the Hampstead Tube are on the other side of the white wall at first-floor level. The ends of two cars are just visible. [1998/76252]

Looking north before the onset of extension work. The future site of Brent station is included. [2004/12843]

This is open country which includes the future site of Hendon Central station. A single figure in the distance appears to be playing golf! [2004/12833]

Country landscape in the Colindale area, 1922. [2004/12993]

South Edgware, 1922. Burnt Oak station and a new road, Watling Avenue, were built in the following year. [2004/12836]

Edgware High Street in around 1910. St Mary's church can be seen, along with a sign indicating the entrance to Edgware Great Northern Railway station. The station opened in 1867 but the slow and infrequent GNR services did little to stimulate growth. [2004/11878]

Children are at play in an Edgware garden. Photographs like this were commissioned for publicity uses. [2004/11869]

This is land acquired for the construction of Edgware station, 1922.
[2004/12842]

This scene includes the future site of Burnt Oak station as it was in April 1922. The Topical Press photographer's log book entry for this negative uses the provisional station name 'Woodstock'.
[1998/78001]

A farmhouse on the site of Hendon Central station, June 1922. All of these 'future site' photographs were commissioned by the Underground Publicity Bureau.[1998/78003]

This is another 'future site', this time for Colindale station. The houses to the left were also purchased and demolished. [1998/78002]

two

Work Begins: June to December 1922

This is the first of a series of photographs taken by a local photographer recording the ceremonial 'cutting of the first sod' which began work on the extension. Lord Ashfield, chairman and managing director of the Underground Group (third left), waits with a group of VIPs for the big event. The striped pole marks the spot. [1998/40581]

Sir Philip Lloyd-Greame, MP and president of the Board of Trade, cuts the first sod on the extension in around 1922. Ceremonies such as this are still common. The task of driving the first pile for the Jubilee line's extension in December 1993 went to the then Prime Minister, John Major. [1998/40880]

Lord Ashfield, Lloyd–Greame's immediate predecessor as president of the Board of Trade, turns the first sod on the extension, to the delight of his audience. [1998/40615]

With the excitement over, the invited guests chat among themselves, while workmen on the far left are beginning the real work. [1998/41092]

Opposite above: A group of workmen with wheelbarrows are poised to begin work, following the ceremonial cutting of the first sod. This serves as a timely reminder of how labour-intensive construction on this scale could be. A booklet published after the opening of the line in August 1924 estimated the total workforce as consisting of 3,000 men. [1998/41025]

Opposite below: Three S-type buses took the press and VIPs to Golders Green for the ceremony. Here they are waiting outside the station to return the crowd to town. A newsreel cameraman surveys the scene from the top of the middle bus. [1998/41020]

Above: Lord Ashfield (right) is chatting to a guest following the sod-cutting ceremony. He does his best to ignore the uninvited audience on the other side of the fence behind him. [1998/40808]

Left: A well-deserved close-up view of the polished ceremonial spade that was employed by both Lloyd-Greame and Ashfield at the 12 June 1922 ceremony. While we do not have this handsome specimen in the museum collection, we do have the scissors used by John Prescott MP at the opening of the Jubilee line extension in 1999. [1998/40619]

The Underground Group's staff architect, Stanley Heaps, photographed in 1943. Heaps designed the five stations on the Northern line extension to Edgware in a Georgian style, with porticos of Portand stone and coupled Doric columns. [1998/75813]

Edgware & Hampstead Extension of London Electric Railway. Opens 1923.

Building the Bridge over the Brent Valley between Brent and Hendon Stations.

The travelling public were kept informed of developments on the new line via a series of posters like this one, showing the beginnings of the bridge over the Brent Valley between Brent and Hendon, one of twelve new bridges built for the extension.

Opposite below: Foundations are built for the railway bridge over Shirehall Lane, between Golders Green and Brent stations, July 1922. Temporary narrow gauge tracks were laid at most sites for the easy removal of spoil and the transport of materials. [1998/78781]

Bridge works at the junction of Woodstock Road and The Riding, looking east towards Golders Green, July 1922. [1998/80725]

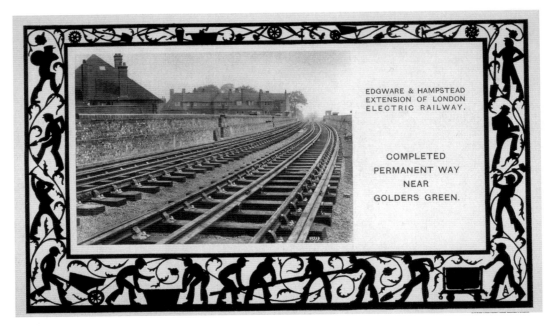

Information posters incorporating photographs of the extension works with decorative graphic borders were posted inside trains. This one shows new track near Golders Green in 1922, with a border by the prolific Italian commercial artist Aldo Cosomati.

The construction of a section of viaduct, west of Hoop Lane, Golders Green, September 1922. [1998/76168]

The same viaduct shown in the previous photograph, between Golders Green Crescent and Hoop Lane, looking towards Golders Green station. [1998/76167]

Edgware & Hampstead Extension of
London Electric Railway. Opens 1923.

At work on the Extension. This machine
mixes many tons of Concrete an hour.

This is an information poster following the progress of the extension, showing a concrete mixer at work, *c.*1922. Eight concrete mixers were employed, with a daily output of 80–100 tons.

The site of Brent station, showing viaduct foundations under construction in background, *c*.1922. [1998/76866]

Edgware & Hampstead Extension of London Electric Railway. Opens 1923.

The first month's work on the Extension at Hoop Lane

A poster illustrates the work completed in the first month of the project at Hoop Lane, Golders Green. It has a decorative border by Edward McKnight-Kauffer.

An American steam shovel helps with the railway cutting through Hendon Park. The Erie company's shovels were reportedly able to dig a ton of earth per minute. [1998/76129]

The excavation of the cutting through Hendon Park continues, with the help of a full gauge steam locomotive, seen from a temporary bridge erected over the tracks. Note the abrupt end of the cutting, not far ahead. [1998/77856]

Work progresses on the building of the Brent Viaduct during October 1922. This photograph includes one of the wooden centrings used to support the arches under construction. The 300ft of viaduct, which was 34ft high, was completed in six months. [1998/76120]

A steam shovel is in use excavating cutting at Hendon. In the foreground a steam locomotive is reversing, pulling trucks filled with spoil away from the site. Workers named the loco *Agnes*, and the steam shovel *Old Bill*. [1998/78007]

Part of Queens Road, by the Hendon Central site, is under construction, with the new road bridge over the line visible beyond. A small steam locomotive pulls a train of hoppers laden with excavated earth. [1998/76148]

The viaduct is taking shape at Hoop Lane, NW11. An electric hoist is used to carry wheelbarrows full of bricks to the top of the section. [1998/76334]

A timber support structure for the railway bridge over Hoop Lane NW11, near Golders Green, with completed viaduct sections to right, December 1922. [1998/78168]

An apparently chaotic construction site at Hendon Central, facing west. The white squares in the background are 'For Sale' signs on the two corner sites at the end of Vivian Avenue, which is as yet unbuilt. [1998/78058]

Golders Green, looking north along Finchley Road. On the right we can see the buffer stops of the original Hampstead line terminus, part of the 'Underground' flowerbed. Also visible is a sign heralding the War Memorial that was to be unveiled on this, the last triangle of 'common land' in the area the following spring. [1998/84500]

The operation of Golders Green station and bus station continued without disruption during the extension work. Route 110, on the right, was renumbered 210 in 1934, and still operates between Finsbury Park and Golders Green, now terminating further north at Brent Cross Shopping Centre. [1999/10462]

GREATER LONDON'S DEVELOPMENT

Before the Underground drove its Railways out to Golders Green there was nothing but green fields. Now there is a considerable Town and a busy population.

New values have been created which stand to the credit of the Underground, though others keep the cash.

Above: Golders Green, looking south-west from the station. A branch of Sainsbury's is visible on the corner of Golders Green Road and Finchley Road, along with at least two estate agents. [1999/3552]

Left: The origins of this poster are obscure; it was printed in 1922, perhaps to pre-empt complaints from residents about the disruption caused by the construction work.

three
January to
August 1923

Early tunnel excavation work from the surface level at Colindale in 1923. [1998/78027]

The excavation of earth along the trackbed at Colindale, with Ruston steam shovel. [1998/78079]

Opposite below: A busy view along Colindeep rail embankment at Colindale. Stacks of steel tunnel segments for a new section of tunnel stand on the left. With two steam shovels and a locomotive to haul spoil in hoppers on sites like this, work progressed quickly. [1998/78055]

Above: Smiling through unpleasant working conditions at Colindale. A narrow gauge steam engine pulling hoppers of spoil is approaching.[1998/78078]

Above and below: These are two views of Finchley Road at Golders Green during the extension work, including the post office, and the London Joint City & Midland bank down the road, with the original Refectory just visible beyond. [1998/17644 and 1998/17620]

The railway bridge at Queens Road, by Hendon Central station, is under construction, 23 March 1923. In the background, sign boards mark out the position of future shop sites on the opposite side of the Circus. [1998/78054]

An aerial view of Hendon Central a few months later, showing the road layout and clusters of new development. [Simmons Aerofilms]

A new road bridge over the extension track at Woodstock Avenue, Golders Green. The level of the road was raised by 7ft to allow the line to pass underneath. [1998/76161]

The site for the new station at Edgware is prepared. [1998/17742]

Above and below: The skeletal structure of Hendon Central station is taking shape, with cutting leading down to beginnings of the Colindeep Tunnel. [1998/76131 and 1998/76119]

Above: The extension was mostly at ground level, but required new sections of tunnel of around 0.5 miles in length between Hendon Central and Colindale. The work took six months of round-the-clock working to complete. [1998/80608]

Below: Men are working on track at Colindale. [1998/80929]

Above: Scaffolding is erected at Colindale, the beginnings of the new station, the second stage of the extension. [1998/76117]

Below: To increase the number of platforms to five, and rearrange the tracks to allow trains to easily reverse or continue towards Edgware, extensive alterations costing around £38,000 were required at Golders Green. [1998/17089]

Work is in progress on the viaduct north of Golders Green, with the original terminus in the background. The workmen are using an electric hoist to transport bricks to the top of the structure. [1998/81533]

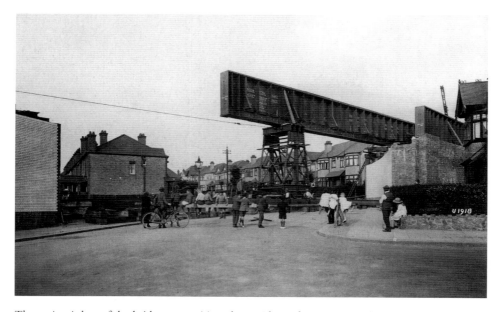

The main girders of the bridge are positioned over Elmcroft Crescent, Golders Green, with few concessions to safety. At nearly 130ft, this was the longest bridge on the extension, weighing 450 tons. [1998/76140]

The station building at Brent looks almost finished from the outside in July 1923, but there is much work still to do. The small shed in the background to the right is marked 'TEA' – a temporary workers' café. [1998/77996]

The brick walls and Portland stone entrance pillars of the Hendon Central station building are enclosed in a framework of wooden scaffolding, five months before opening. [1998/78018]

A poster showing Hendon Central station, the new bridge over Queens Road, and an area marked off for the new roundabout. A booklet, published to mark the opening of this section of the line, refers to the area as 'the Piccadilly Circus of North West London'. [image only: 1998/78040]

This is the basic framework for the future station at Burnt Oak, an entirely new district to the east of the main Edgware Road. The Underground Group also built a new road to the station, Watling Avenue, as part of the project, in tandem with the London County Council, who were soon to begin building their Watling Estate nearby. [1998/78038]

Substantial alterations were made to Golders Green station to facilitate the extension of the line, without interruptions to regular services. Here, timber platforms are being removed. A gate tube stock train can be seen through the bracing on the right, while Golders Green depot is on the left. [1998/16661]

Above: The placement of the 250-ton main girder structure of the railway bridge over Finchley Road in 1923, immediately north of the old Hampstead Tube terminus at Golders Green. [1998/76143]

Below: Part of the new railway bridge over Golders Green Crescent is being hoisted into position before a small crowd of onlookers. [1998/76082]

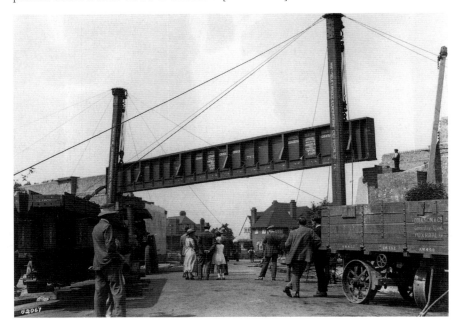

Above: These are four of the thousands of men who worked on the extension at Golders Green. Although one holds a pneumatic drill, the pick and shovel against the wall beside them give a better indication of the heavy labour-intensive work. [1998/16657]

Below: Finchley Road at Golders Green, looking towards Finchley, with the new bridge in place. Original cataloguing gives the name of the road as Regents Park Road, which now starts further east. [1998/76144]

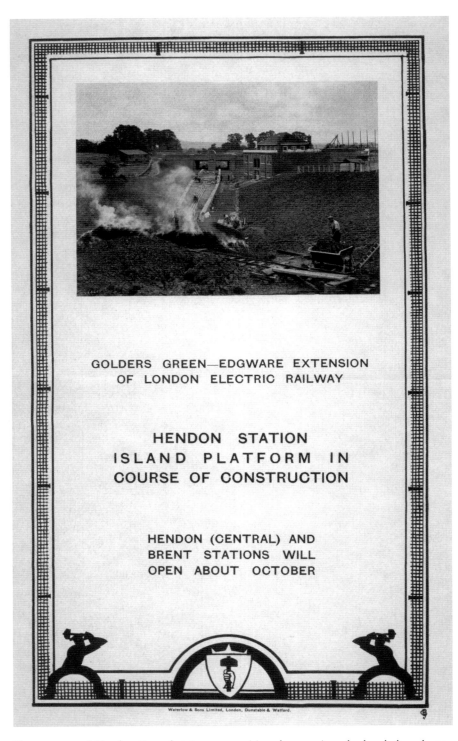

The area around Hendon Central station was envisioned as a major suburban hub, and was promoted accordingly. [image only: 1998/78019]

four
September to December 1923

These three photographs were intended to be joined together as a panorama of the beginnings of Central Circus, Hendon NW4, in September 1923. The small final image below gives an idea of the panoramic effect. The first image shows the almost complete façade of Hendon Central station and the bridge over Queens Road. The second shows gravel and brick-fragments, laid out in a circular pattern – the area later occupied by the Central Circus roundabout, replaced with a conventional junction in the 1960s. The third image shows the new buildings at the end of Vivian Avenue under construction, including the Westminster (NatWest) bank on the left side. [1998/75586, 1998/75587, 1998/75456 & 1998/97836]

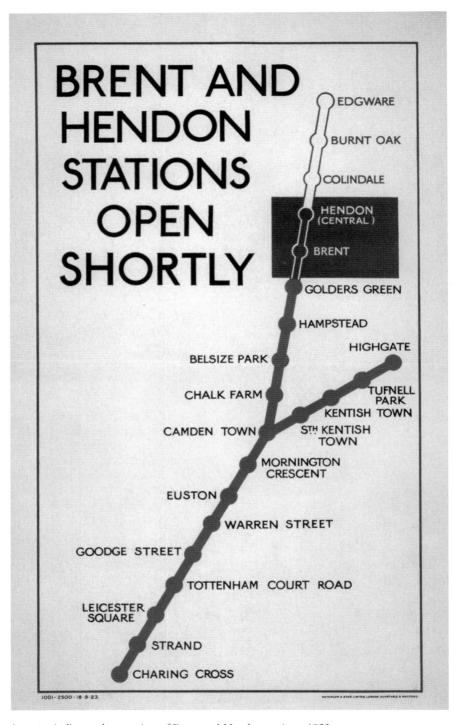

A poster indicates the opening of Brent and Hendon stations, 1923.

The construction of the signal cabin, which stood at the northerly end of the platforms at Hendon Central station until the 1960s. [1998/78009]

Brent station is close to completion a month before opening. It was renamed Brent Cross in 1976 after the opening of the shopping centre nearby. [1998/77888]

Above: The interior of the finished signal cabin Hendon 'AB', with an electric signal frame and illuminated diagram at Hendon Central station. The hanging diagram illustrates the position of a train as it enters and leaves the station. Underground Group literature for the period proudly announced that the signalling on the new line was 'All Electric, with the latest type of track circuit' and Daylight Colour light signals. [1998/81148]

Above: Hendon Central station booking hall in 1923, an area of 3,250 sq. ft including the vestibule, is shown a month before opening. The free-standing timber ticket offices were known as passimeters. [1998/81016]

Below: Brent station on the occasion of the electrification of this section of the extension, only a week before opening to the public. A 1906 gate tube stock train pulls up to the platform. [1998/78106]

Opposite below: The electricity for the extension was supplied direct from the Underground's own Chelsea power station, at 11,000 volts AC, and was converted to 600 volts DC at three new substations along the line. In the 1980s part of the Hendon substation, shown here, was converted for use as a store and office for the museum photograph collections. [1998/76206]

Above: This is an aerial view of the construction site at Edgware, 1923. As the first stage of the extension neared completion, work further north continued. [Simmons Aerofilms]

Below: Construction is underway at Edgware station. This is the view from the left side of forecourt. [1998/77911]

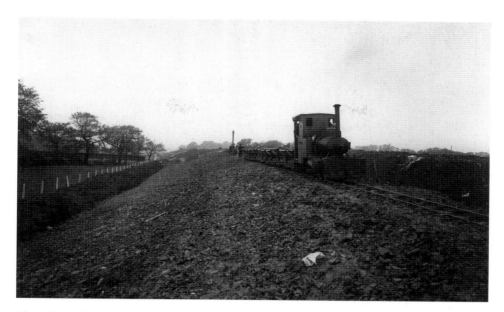

Above: A small steam locomotive is pulling a train of hoppers on a temporary track, near Colindale. Around 50,000 cubic yards of earth were excavated from the steep cuttings approaching the station. [1998/81163]

Below: Men are at work behind the tunnelling shield and rotary excavator in the Colindeep tunnel, removing the spoil which is carried away by the conveyor belt. [1998/76779]

Golders Green station, its forecourt and busy bus station, just before the opening of the extension. The forecourt, viewed from the roof of the Hippodrome theatre, is crowded with B-type, S-type and K-type buses. The new War Memorial is clearly visible on the top left, with the tracks of the extension disappearing into the top right. [1999/20305]

Planned for October, the first section of the extension was finished in late November, 1923.

This page and the following: OPENING DAY – 19 November 1923

A ceremony to mark the switching-on of the current to the first section of the Edware extension, by the local Conservative MP Sir Philip Lloyd-Greame, on the platform of Golders Green Green. Lloyd-Greame, whom you may remember as 'cutter of the first sod', changed his surname to Cunliffe-Lister the following year, and became a prominent and successful politician, earning a succession of honours, and ending his days as Earl of Swinton. [1998/40576]

Sir Philip Lloyd-Greame, leaning out of the driver's cab of the 'Hendon Special' inaugural train at Golders Green. [1998/40756]

George Lloyd-Greame, the local MP's young son, gets in on the act. He does not seem to have followed his father into politics. [1998/40526]

Lord Ashfield stands with Inspector Smith on the platform at Brent station, by the cab of the 'Hendon Special'. [1998/84708]

The view from tracks at Golders Green looking north, on the opening day of the first section of the extension to Hendon Central, 1923. [1998/80645]

This Brent, so typical of Stanley Heaps' smaller stations on the extension, decorated for the occasion of its opening to the public. [1998/81022]

An expectant crowd waits behind the closed gates of Hendon Central station on opening day. A policeman is on hand in case anyone were to get over-excited. [1998/85108]

One step closer to the platforms at Hendon Central. A man in a raincoat and felt hat is about to become the first passenger to purchase a ticket from one of the two passimeters. [1998/79102]

The first passenger train at Hendon Central – 3 p.m., Monday 19 November 1923. Standard tube stock trains like this would run on the line until their gradual replacement with 1938 tube stock a quarter of a century later. [1998/79100]

Hendon Central, decorated with flags for its opening. [1999/20144]

A ceremonial first train of 1923 standard stock at the platform of Brent station, with the Underground Group chairman, Lord Ashfield. [1998/77952]

The booking hall vestibule at Hendon Central station, with characteristic chessboard floor tiling, and glazed doors to the main booking hall. [1998/61919]

A lower angled view of the Hendon Central booking hall, showing the clerestory windows and light fittings, which are common to all of Heaps' extension designs. [1998/61922]

The platforms at Hendon Central in 1924. [1998/71794]

The London-bound platform at Brent. No photographs were taken at the opening, but some years later all its original features remain intact. [1998/69471]

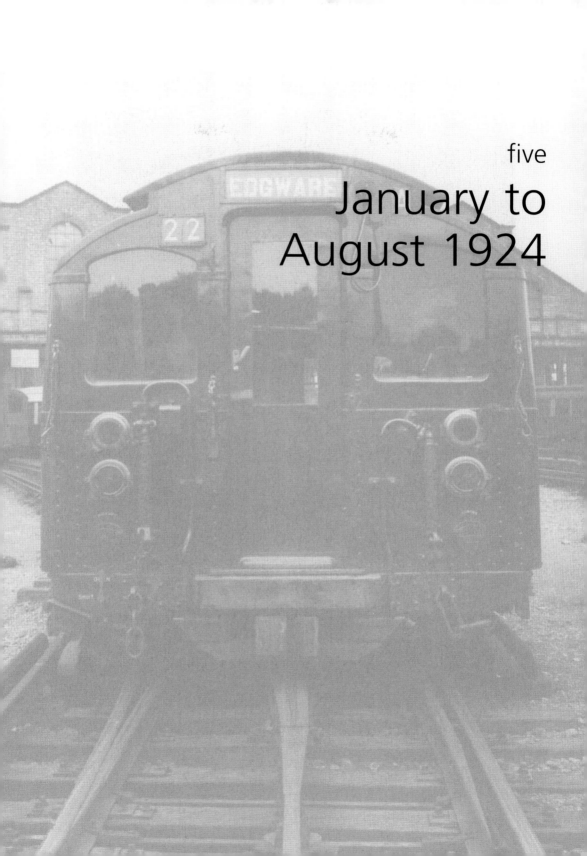

five

January to August 1924

Golders Green station in 1924, seen from track level on the Hampstead side, showing all five platforms. [1998/80996]

The new London-bound platform at Golders Green. [1998/80784]

The new tunnels from Hendon Central to Colindale, with much work still to do. [1998/78083]

The Great Northern Railway bridge over the extension line at Edgware. [1998/76134]

A carefully chosen vision of 'Old Hendon', Brent Street, dominated by Christ Church on the right. A small sign on the lamppost nearby indicates the way to Hendon Central station via Heriot Road. [1998/14397]

This shows more of 'Old Hendon', further away from the station. The house dominating the image is identified in the photographer's log book as 'St Dunstans'. [1998/17255]

The tunnel portals, 'island' platform and signal box at Hendon Central station. Known initially as Hendon (Central), the brackets were soon dropped. [1998/75454]

Colindale station, described in the Underground literature as, 'a red brick building of Georgian style, square in plan with a clerestory and a pyramidical red tiled roof … [and] a Doric colonnade-portico of Portland stone.' [1998/80599]

Above and below: Watling Avenue, the road from Edgware Road down to the new Burnt Oak station site, was built as part of the extension, and continued on to Mill Hill by the local authority. [1998/80934 and 1998/80211]

A new 1923 standard tube stock motor car at Golders Green, described in the booklet published to mark the opening of the extension as, 'embodying the most advanced improvements in underground rolling stock – luxurious seating, with additional cross-seats; brilliant yet soft lighting; additional doors, and all doors controlled and operated by the Guard.' [1998/80911]

HENDON—EDGWARE EXTENSION
RAILWAY.

YOU WANT A HOME
SEEK IT AT
BRENT OR HENDON

UNDERGROUND

NEW HOUSES AT HENDON.　　　JUNE 1924.

Waterlow & Sons Limited, London, Dunstable & Watford.

A 1924 poster advertising new housing in Hendon. During 1923/24, more than 2,000 new houses and shops were built or approved in the area, some of which are shown in the following sequence of photographs.

Empty unfinished shops flanking the newly opened Westminster bank, stretch into Vivian Avenue, opposite Hendon Central station. [1998/17193]

New houses in Elliot Road, Hendon NW4. [1998/17187]

Park Road, Hendon NW4. [1998/17185]

One side of Rundell Crescent, Hendon NW4.[1998/17180]

Rundell Crescent and beyond. It is reminiscent of a twentieth-century version of George Cruikshank's famous cartoon of 1829, *The March of Bricks and Mortar!* [1998/17354]

Hendon Central station in 1924, after the completion of the line to Edgware. The shop unit to the right of the entrance is still empty. [1998/84428]

Cable laying between Colindale and Edgware. A steam crane lifts a reel of cable off an open wagon. The number of men on hand reminds us how labour-intensive the work is. [1998/77989]

Workmen are laying tracks at the approach to Edgware station. [1998/80846]

A new rail depot was also required at the Edgware terminus to accommodate twenty–eight cars. It was designed to fit in with Stanley Heaps' station architecture. [1998/80925]

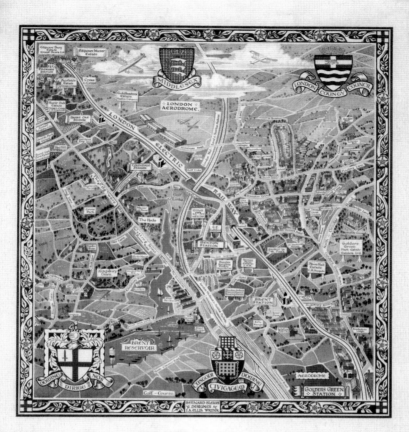

SEEK A HOME OF YOUR OWN
IN THE NEW COUNTRY

FROM	TO CHARING CROSS			TO MOORGATE		
	Journey Time	Single Fare	Quarterly Season	Journey Time	Single Fare	Quarterly Season
	minutes	d.	s. d.	minutes	d.	s. d.
EDGWARE .	34	8	62/6	34	9	67/6
BURNT OAK .	32	8	62/6	32	9	67/6
COLINDALE . .	29	7	57/6	29	8	62/6
HENDON (Central)	26	6	52/6	26	7	57/6
BRENT . . .	24	6	52/6	24	7	57/6

A stylised map of the country covered by the extension, with journey times and fares to
Charing Cross and Moorgate, by Bernard Sleigh.

Construction at Edgware station, looking south along the central island platform. The new sheds are on the left. [1998/80848]

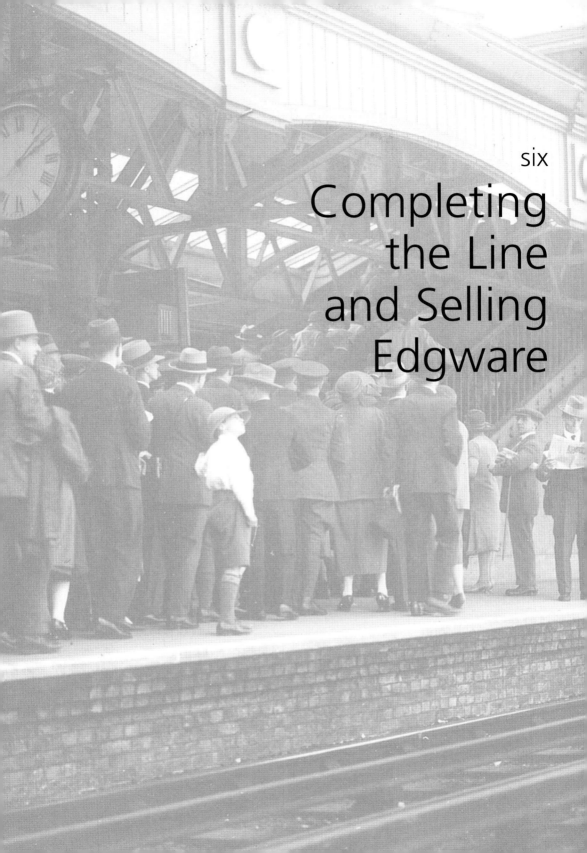

six

Completing the Line and Selling Edgware

Hendon Central. A week before the opening to Edgware, men are still working on the track cabling. The earlier station name signs have been replaced by the familiar 'tombstone' style and the brackets in the name are gone. [1998/78008]

Experimental running of a two-car train at Colindale in early August 1924. [1998/80816]

An aerial view of Colindale station and the track of the new railway, looking towards Hendon. The Aerodrome, now home to the RAF Museum, is visible in the top left corner. [Simmons Aerofilms]

Colindale station. Delays due to strike action meant that Colindale and Edgware opened to the public before the last of the building work had finished. [1998/78062]

Above: A completed but lonely Colindale station, 1924. [1998/73783]

Below: An experimental six-car train near Edgware.

Edgware station, platforms and canopy, behind schedule with only a week to go. [1998/77988]

Edgware station and forecourt before completion – a composite of two negatives to show the whole of Heaps' building, described in company literature as, 'altogether unique in design as far as local railway stations are concerned. Externally it is Italian in feeling, comprising a centre and wings which form three sides of a quadrangle'. [1998/77905]

Printed just before the opening of Edgware station, this poster by Walter Spradbery shows
Edgware as more of a country day-trip destination than a new place to live.

A contrasting poster from later in the same year emphasises the fact that Edgware is a well-connected local hub. The map by Charles Shepherd shows the catchment area of Edgware as stretching as far as Amersham and St Albans, and is marked with the bus routes that lead to it.

The gentlemen of the press arrive for a free lunch and a preview of Edgware station and the extension as whole. The roof is clearly unfinished. [1998/79084]

A lavish refreshment tent is set up for the press preview of Edgware station. Note the many wine and champagne bottles in the foreground and the string quartet at the back. [1998/77983]

The new car sheds and sidings at Edgware. The 'shed' on the left side is the canopy roof over the station platforms. [1998/80665]

Underground publicity for the extension stressed the 'country joys within reach of the city' angle, much like the Metropolitan Railway's promotion of 'Metro–Land', but tried simultaneously to emphasise the modernity of the new line. The photograph on this poster shows completed track near Burnt Oak.

A four-car train of 1923 standard tube stock at Golders Green, heading south into the tunnel towards Hampstead. [1998/80730]

The platforms of Hendon Central station, with a three-car train headed for Edgware. [U52711]

A typical message told in bold graphics by artist William Kermode, complemented by the words of the seventeenth-century poet, Abraham Cowley, reads, 'I never had any other desire so strong and so like to covetousness as that one which I have had always, that I might be Master of a small House and a Large Garden, with moderate conveniences joined to them'.

Early posters promoting Edgware were able to characterise it as an 'old world village', but this image was not sustainable as the population of the area grew. The photograph in this poster was taken a few yards down the road on the same day as the next two images, which give a less idyllic impression of Edgware at this time.

The High Street in 'Old Edgware', a few hundred yards from the new railway terminus. [1998/17087]

Edgware High Street at the junction with Station Road, leading to the new railway station. [1998/14239]

An earlier view of Edgware from the Publicity Bureau's 'Country Scenes' files. An open-top tram operated by the Metropolitan Electric Tramways is approaching the Chandos Arms public house. [2004/11828]

Above: The future site for a parade of shops at Station Road, Edgware, seen from the entrance of the station, looking across the island garden, and framed by a pair of Portland stone columns. [1998/14402]

Left: A slightly later view of the colonnade at Edgware. [2004/12178]

Opposite page: The posters commissioned to promote Edgware are numerous and varied. This 1924 example by Helen Bryce elaborates on an exaggerated, and not entirely serious, fantasy of suburban life in the style of a Victorian embroidery sampler.

LIVE AT EDGWARE
and *LIVE* !

LIVE IN EDGWARE

Everyone wants a happy home. You will find happiness
and real comfort at Edgware. So many attractive
and inexpensive houses, fitted with every
modern improvement are being built
there. Why not buy one
and live in the country
economically?

Don't let the
distance make you
hesitate. Fast electric trains,
running at frequent intervals, will
take you to and from the City and West
End in a little over half an hour. This gives
you a healthy country life within easy reach of London.

WORK IN LONDON

M4/175·25   *Service Advertising*

Print advertising,
arguably a less subtle
medium, was also
employed. Designers
– in this case Aldo
Cosomati – often
played with the
Underground's
'roundel' symbol to
make a point.

Construction at Burnt Oak was the most directly affected by strikes in the workforce, which delayed its opening until late October 1924. At this point only a small temporary structure was finished, to be replaced by a proper station 'on the lines of Colindale, when traffic has been developed'. [1998/74589]

The full Heaps design for Burnt Oak was completed without fanfare in 1928, to coincide with the beginnings of the London County Council's nearby Watling Estate. The station name was also altered to Burnt Oak (Watling) for a time. [1998/74592]

A view of Burnt Oak platform, clearly showing the truncated station building. There were few local residents at this time. [1999/8151]

Left: At the time of writing, Burnt Oak is one of several Underground stations being extensively remodelled. Readers can rest assured that the original wood-framed enamel station name signs, like this one seen in October 2001, will eventually be reinstated.

Opposite below: House building at Elmer Gardens, near Edgware station. A number of estate agents' boards can be seen in front of three of the houses on the right. [1998/16649]

Above: This poster, 'New Works' by Fred Taylor, shows an idealised extension station in the style of Colindale and Burnt Oak, in the background of a suburban building site.

Underground posters were printed to publicise flying displays at Hendon as early as 1913, indicating the buses from Golders Green to the Hendon site. This example is by R.P. Gossop and is from 1926.

Above and opposite: The proximity of the new station to the aerodrome, requisitioned by the Air Ministry in 1923 and now home to the RAF Museum, allowed huge crowds to reach the air shows for the first time. [2004/19310, 2004/19311, 2004/19312]

Above: The completed new rail depot at Edgware, with an array of 1923 standard tube stock trains. [1998/56285]

Below: A side entrance to Brent station. This was later accessed by a short alleyway from Highfield Avenue, built soon after. [1998/56440]

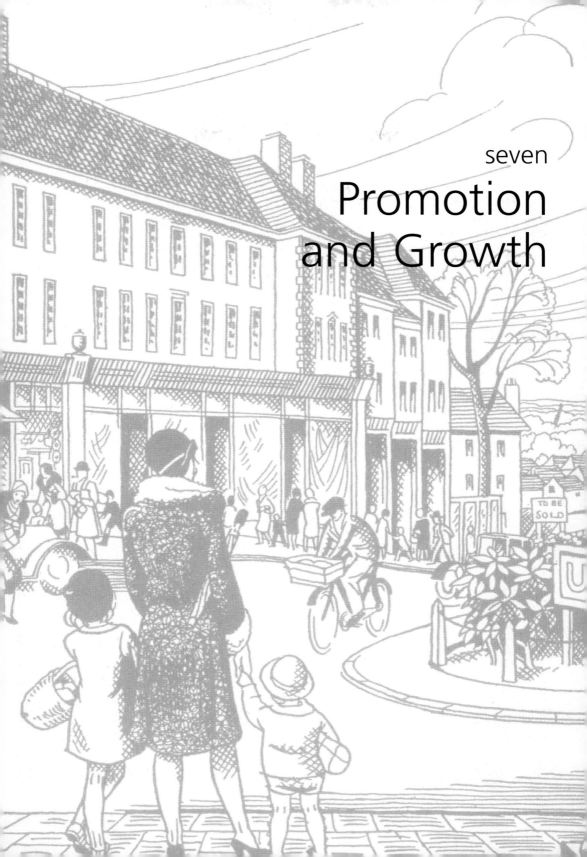

seven

Promotion and Growth

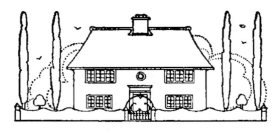

A LITTLE HOUSE
AND A GARDEN
AT
EDGWARE

COSTS FROM £900 TO £1,600

Or you can buy the land and build a house to your own design. A Building Plot will cost from £7 10s. to £10 per foot.

Edgware is situated 200 feet above ordnance datum. Main water-supply. Electricity: 7d. per unit for Lighting, $2\frac{1}{2}$d. per unit for power. Gas: 10·4d. per therm. Rates: 8s. 5d. in the £.

AND A TRAIN TO TOWN EVERY 8 MINUTES

Cheap Return Tickets are issued to Edgware on Saturdays and Sundays from most Underground Stations. Why not go there next week-end and stake your claim in Edgware Garden Suburb.

M2/19/26

By 1926 advertisements could no longer use images of the countryside to represent Edgware. Artists switched to illustrations of houses and considerations of cash rather than of country living.

THERE ARE STREETS
★ ★ ★ ★ ★ ★ ★
AND STREETS

LIVE AT
EDGWARE
ON THE

M1 '21/'26

Edgware station, March 1926. At this point most of the arcade shop units are still empty, apart from the inevitable estate agents. The bus on the right, a K-type, is on route 140 to Pinner. [1999/20600]

The booking hall at Edgware, 1926. Broadly similar to others on the extension, the terminus station was distinguished by the addition of polished oak woodwork and bronze fittings. [1998/61923]

New suburbs spread out across Hendon, and are seen from the platform at Brent. [1998/16447]

Edgware Road at the junction with Watling Avenue. Burnt Oak station is indicated by hanging signs pointing to the right. Note the lack of paving on this side of the road. [1998/13496]

House building at Burnt Oak, February 1927. These are the beginnings of the LCC's Watling Estate. [1998/16344]

Further developments at Burnt Oak, June 1927. [1998/16305]

Frank Pick defined a station as, 'an inviting doorway in an architectural setting that cannot be missed by the casual pedestrian'. Heaps' design for Edgware certainly fits that description. The station is seen here on Saturday 3 July 1926. [1999/20702]

Edgware station and rail depot, seen from the air, September 1926. [Simmons Aerofilms]

By 1930, promotion for Edgware, as in this example by Christine Jackson, seems to be emphasising shopping rather than home buying, although a tiny 'to be sold' sign is included in the distance.

The booking hall of Brent station, October 1927. This picture shows a full complement of features typical of most of the extension stations – wooden passimeters, chequerboard floor tiling, clerestory windows and hexagonal light shades. [1998/62714]

Colindale booking hall, distinguished by many of the same architectural features, January 1928. [1998/61940]

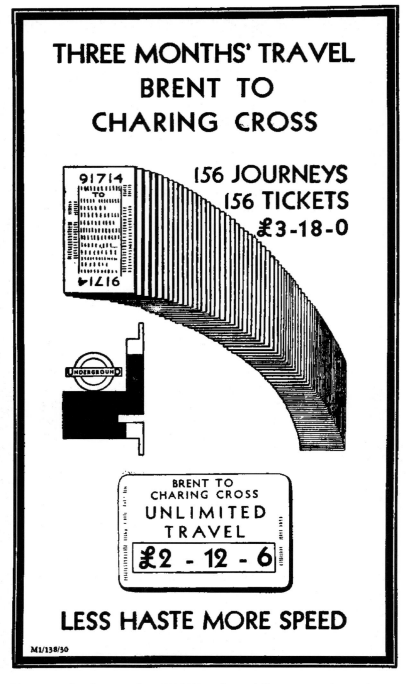

Two press advertisements from 1929/30, and two different approaches to the promotion of season tickets on the Edgware extension. The first stresses only the monetary benefits in graphical form, while the other emphasises the extra free leisure travel using text only.

MR. BLYTHE, OF HENDON

Mr. Blythe lives in one of those new houses near the Tube station. His office is at Charing Cross, and he saves £1 5s. 6d. a quarter by using a Season Ticket for his twelve business journeys every week.

Most Saturday afternoons you'll find him on the Hampstead golf-links. This journey costs him nothing. Occasionally he takes Mrs. Blythe to a theatre. Again his journey costs nothing. On Sundays he goes to a West End church. Another free journey. And what he saves in fares he puts into the plate. In the afternoon he rides to Hampstead, and takes his dog over the Heath. His own journey costs nothing.

Neither does he pay fares when he goes to see friends at Belsize Park, or to his club in Leicester Square; or to buy furniture in Tottenham Court Road, or clothes in Oxford Street. Even when he visits his dentist in the Strand it costs him nothing —in fares, at any rate. And when he departs, on his summer holidays, it costs him nothing to get to the starting-point at Euston.

Mr. Blythe's Season Ticket gives him the use of thirteen intermediate stations on the line without any extra charge. What is the full value of the privilege in a year? It depends only upon how much he uses it.

Now put yourself in his shoes. Perhaps there are even wider advantages awaiting you?—if you take a Season Ticket on the

M1/68/29

Above: Hendon Central station and the 'Piccadilly Circus of North West London'. In the six years since opening, the station has been built over with flats and connected to buildings on each side, although there are still vacant commercial premises on the right. [1998/56413]

Below: An aerial view of Central Circus in 1930, showing the full extent of development in the years since goats and golfers roamed the area. The plot, which was later occupied by the cinema – and subsequently taken over by a huge gym complex – is still empty. [Simmons Aerofilms]

Although the useum photo collection is primarily a historic archive of black and white images, we continue to record the activities of Transport for London, adding to the collection with colour and digital photography. The modern photographs in this section were taken in October 2001, as part of a programme to record the entire Underground network for a museum database project.

Above: Golders Green; the main building and booking hall opening onto the bus station has been changed around many times since opening, not least in the last twenty years, but the roof line of the original building can still be seen in this photograph from 2001. A passimeter installed in 1923 was acquired by London's Transport Museum in 1998. [2001/52145]

A view of the platform at Golders Green station, showing the 1923 platform canopies. gates. [2001/52147]

Above: Brent station was renamed Brent Cross in 1976 when the shopping centre opened. Aside from the removal of passimeters and addition of ticket gates applied across the whole tube network, the station has not been radically altered. The forecourt, once a mini bus station, had been given over to parking by the time of this photograph in 2001. [2001/52166]

Below: Brent Cross booking hall, with new ticket gates. [2001/52168]

In September 1988, a removal van driver fell asleep at the wheel and drove into one of the Portland stone columns at Hendon Central. It was fully restored the following year. [2001/15186]

The building has seen relatively few changes since the 1920s, most in the main booking hall area, and is generally regarded as the best surviving Stanley Heaps station. [2001/52154]

The platforms at Hendon Central, with modern lighting and signage. [2001/52162]

The original Colindale station took a direct hit in the first wave of Second World War air raids in September 1940. It was replaced by a temporary structure soon afterwards, but was not properly rebuilt until 1962. A recent architect's appraisal of the 1960s building described the entrance as 'emphatically horizontal'. [2001/52179]

Platforms with modern signage are combined with original hanging platform number signs. [2001/52185]

Surprisingly, the 1962 booking hall at Colindale does manage to retain some of the look of the original, albeit with different materials and finishes, and the ubiquitous brushed steel ticket gates. [2001/52182]

Up to this point in October 2001, alterations to Burnt Oak were restricted to the installation of new ticketing systems in the booking hall. As this book goes to press, the station is six months into a major modernisation programme to upgrade lighting, customer information and security. [2001/52173]

Burnt Oak booking hall, with some original features intact. [2001/52175]

A view of the platform, with the original station name sign and bench unit, to be reinstated after platform resurfacing. [2001/52169]

Edgware in 2001. A shadow of its former self, the station lost its east wing in 1938 during preliminary work for the ill-fated extension north to Elstree, and the west wing fifty years later to a new bus station and shopping arcade. [2001/52170]

The booking hall at Edgware, with the usual alterations. [2001/52174]

Edgware's platforms today, with nothing but the roof left from 1924. [2001/52171]

Related titles published by Tempus

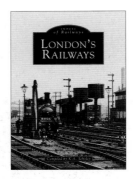

London's Railways

KEITH SCHOLEY

London's Railways gives a unique insight into the history of the railways in the Capital. This book brings the classic age of rail travel to life and demonstrates just how much London was, and still is, dependent on the shimmering ribbons of steel that have penetrated both over and under the city from all directions.

0 7524 1605 7

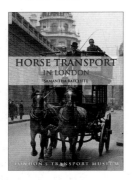

The Metropolitan Railway

DAVID BOWNES

The Metropolitan was the world's first underground railway. Opened in 1863, by 1900 the network reached almost fifty miles into the countryside northwest of Baker Street and creating suburban 'Metro-land'. The Met can still boast the furthest destination on the London Underground today.

0 7524 3105 6

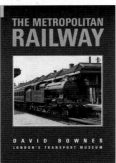

Horse Transport in London

SAMANTHA RATCLIFFE

From the waterways to the motorcar London's transport underwent a huge revolution. This collection of images examines the vehicles that changed London's transport in the Victorian and Edwardian eras through to the impact petrol and the motorcar had on the scene, from the horse cabs of 1823 through to the last horse tram to ride London's streets.

0 7524 3458 6

Women at Work on London's Transport 1905-1978

ANNA ROTONDARO

The outbreak of the First World War necessitated the development of the then small female workforce into a major force that would rise to even greater prevalence in the Second World War, changing the employment sector forever. This collection of images charts the history of women at work on London's transport from a typist in 1905 to a tube driver in the mid-1970s.

0 7524 3265 6

If you are interested in purchasing other books published by Tempus, or in case you have difficulty finding any Tempus books in your local bookshop, you can also place orders directly through our website

www.tempus-publishing.com